UNNAMEABLE

SELECTED POEMS *of*

Anna Gual

Translated from Catalan by

AKaiser

Zephyr Press

Published in 2025 by
Zephyr Press www.zephyrpress.org

Cover detail from the painting *Autoretrat embarassada* [Self-portrait, pregnant] (1966–1967) by Mari Chordà. Reproduced by kind permission of Mari Chordà and Museu Nacional d'Art de Catalunya, purchased with funds provided by the Friends of the Museu Nacional d'Art de Catalunya Foundation, 2019.

Book design by typeslowly
Printed in Michigan by Cushing Malloy

We acknowledge with gratitude the financial support of the Massachusetts Cultural Council, the Institut Ramon Llull and The Academy of American Poets with funds from the Amazon Literary Partnership Poetry Fund.

Mass Cultural Council

Zephyr Press, a non-profit arts and education 501(c)(3) organization, publishes literary titles that foster a deeper understanding of cultures and languages. Zephyr Press books are distributed to the trade by Consortium Book Sales and Distribution [www.cbsd.com].

Cataloguing-in publication data is available from the Library of Congress.

ISBN 978-1-938890-36-9

CONTENTS

DEDICATION

To dear open heart and translation collaborator,
Ngũgĩ wa Thiong'o (1938–2025), a practitioner of,
believer in, and voice for translation,
the language of languages.

Translator's Introduction

> *I'm all these words, all these strangers, this dust of words with no grounds for their settling . . .*
>
> —Samuel Beckett, *The Unnameable*

Anna Gual is a Catalan poet who arrived on the scene in 2012 via her blog, *I'm not falling, I am throwing myself,* winner of the Best Blog Written in Catalan. Since that time, she has become a prize-winning poet and is now the author of eight collections. She has been lauded critically while reaching a faithful pan-European audience as she gives voice to her gifts of sensing, feeling and expressing awe of, and in, the beguiling quotidian, which is everything, if our eyes are open. For Gual, the universe is a vast topography, and her urge to render it is her compass rose.

Born in Catalonia's wine country—a region imprinting her work and that the poet continues to call home—Gual studied audiovisual creation and cultural management in Barcelona. Catalonia is a region of Spain where most people are raised bilingual in Catalan and Spanish. Catalan is one of Spain's four official languages, the others being Basque, Galician and Spanish. To the ever-present, articulated, or not, question: Why do you write in Catalan? she, like many of her generation born after the Francoist dictatorship (1939–1975), replies: "I am Catalan. Why wouldn't I write in Catalan?" Unlike, for example, the outstanding poet-translator Francesc Parcerisas, who, like many of his generation, having spent half their lives under the regime, ran the real risk of choosing to write in their first language. Gual's generation, thanks to the return of democracy in Spain and the trailblazing work of Catalan wordsmiths like Parcerisas, is now free to turn their attention elsewhere.

To experience Gual's words is to embark with her on a quest. An inventive searching towards the liminal; towards omnipresence and elusive horizons—both horizontal and vertical; towards dirt-laden construction and de-construction sites; towards an often willingly unhinged coursing through time, rivers, and electrical currents, to say nothing of one's own veins. In the world of Catalan literature, she is an integral literary force, or, as poet Miriam Reyes states, "one of the most [...] respected, prize-winning and read of her generation." She forms part of a Catalan poetry lineage that includes Gemma Gorga, Antònia Vicens, Màrius Sampere, Francesc Garriga, Míriam Cano, and Mireia Calafell. The anthology, *Women Writers in Catalan, The (H) Original Generation, half a century of Catalan poetry, from May 1968 to 2018*, (Raig Verd, Barcelona, 2018), fleshes this out for the interested reader, as does, more specifically for this century, "Catalan women poets of the 21st century have a doctoral thesis" (https://educationalevidence.com/en/catalan-women-poets-of-the-21st-century-have-a-doctoral-thesis/).

Beginning with her first book, *Implosions* (2008), to the seventh, *Ameba* (2020), winner of the Rosa Leveroni Prize, and her 2022 *Les ocultacions*, winner of the Miquel de Palol Prize, Gual has demonstrated her attempts at and genius for noticing and communicating life in all of its unexpectedness, whether she is exploring—excavating if need be—the micro to the macro, speleological interiors to faraway exteriors and pushing further still, from invisibility to visibility and back again. She remains determined to break down barriers, or to show us the folly of believing in them at all—between human beings and the so-called natural world, between and within bodies, or in the flesh and blood of language itself. Now joining previous collections translated into French, Italian, and Spanish, *Unnameable*, is the first book of Gual's work to be translated into English.

* * *

Despite significant experiential distances, there are echoes in Gual's vigorous oeuvre of the Austrian Ingeborg Bachmann, Argentine Alejandra Pizarnik, and Belarusian Valzhyna Mort, with their passions for, and frustrations within, the constrictions of language, alongside the comprehension that this may be (almost) all we have. Reciprocal, and not, at the same time. The intellect to observe and admit the world, the will to attempt to surpass or rupture, to create worlds, while accepting, if not greeting with open arms, the accompanying birth pangs.

Ingeborg Bachmann, "Always to live among words":

> Always to live among words, whether one wants to or not,
> Always to be alive, full of words about life,
> as if words were alive, as if life meant words.
>
> But it's otherwise, believe me.[1]

Or, from Alejandra Pizarnik's prose work, "[All night I hear the noise of water sobbing.]":

> All night I write luminous messages, messages of rain, all night someone checks for me and I check for someone.[2]

---

1. Ingeborg Bachmann, "[Always to live among words]," trans., Peter Filkins, in *Darkness Spoken: The Collected Poems of Ingeborg Bachmann* (Brookline, MA: Zephyr Press, 2006).

2. Alejandra Pizarnik, "[All night I hear the noise of water sobbing.]," trans. Patricio Ferrari and Forrest Gander, in *The Galloping Hour: French Poems*, ed. by Patricio Ferrari (New York: New Directions Publishing, 2018).

Valzhyna Mort's "Belarusian i":

> we fought the summer heat the winter snow
> when we discovered we ourselves were the language
> and our tongues were removed we started talking with our eyes[3]

And Anna Gual, in turn:

> Sprouts
>
> In between letter and letter
> so much grass is born
> which I won't mow down.
>
> I've returned to digging up meanings,
> to tauten words by joining them.

All women poets, they might have been—or might still be—asked: by what right do you unearth the meanings of anything? Though, yes, we might say that today's woman-poet is a (mostly) acceptable creature. But truly, the pause it gives when considering how recent this liberty with language is for women—and it is, of course, by no means uniform nor universal. It seems to me that women have always had to strive to create modes of expression and that these four poets are no exception, only exceptional in how they managed or manage to do it; that is, how they bypass dogma, and not without cost, to compose a musical grammar that is each wildly their own.

At the age of twelve, Ingeborg Bachmann witnessed the Nazis march into her small town. Losing her democratic nation and having her language co-opted for barbarism, she carried the attendant shame, and

---

3. Valzhyna Mort, "[Belarussian i]," trans. Elizabeth Oehlkers Wright and Franz Wright in *Factory of Tears* (Port Townsend, WA: Copper Canyon Press, 2008).

guilt, within her for the rest of her life. In the war's aftermath, could poetry, indeed, still be written at all, let alone in German? She took on this responsibility of being a German-language writer, of trying to answer Adorno's question. She knew she had to create a new mode of language, a subject she and Paul Celan, her close friend for most of their adult lives, both wrestled with until the end.

Alejandra Pizarnik was born in Argentina, a mid-20th c. majority Catholic country, to Jewish immigrants from modern day Ukraine, and so lived within at least two linguistic and cultural influences. She struggled with a stutter as well as depression for much of her adolescent life and was diagnosed with schizophrenia as an adult. One can read the generous critical work on her writing, and imagine for oneself her perceived "outsider" status with life and language—often manifesting itself, all the same, in self-censorship on many fronts: physical, emotional, political, private, and, as we might now say based on her clinical diagnosis, neurological. From her life and language, Pizarnik left us a flaring and far-reaching oeuvre, cultivating therein, as she said, "the art of unreason."

Valzhyna Mort's relationship with language, one can surmise, has been greatly influenced by the forced map of her exile from the Belarusian dictatorship and the experiences of that land and its people which helped to shape her, including, but not exclusively, the powerful presence of her grandmother. Her travels are both interior and exterior, abstract and concrete, as she departed from her homeland and came to live in the US, all the while having as companions Belarusian, Russian, and English in her personal and political life of poetry, and translated verse. She, too, creates echoing incantations and images with her work.

Gual is partner in these poets' circumnavigations, indefatigably *en voyage* within language/s, and ineluctably, as she writes in "Profanity," with tools in hand:

> I didn't want a map.
> I wanted a machete to clear a path

* * *

As a child, Gual's grandfather took her into the vineyards to ingrain in her a sense of agri-viti-time. For all her curiosity and wanderings, then, she is rooted in this specific landscape, living and working where she was born and, as her grandfather, working in and knowing the entangled vines and their cyclical joy. Gual limns what was once called the natural world, pastoral or otherwise, in ways unique to her: the intimate experience with soil, vineyards, seeds, flowers, fields, sun, and snow. As an extension, there is the natural world of her family, generations before and into the future. In short, the poet's exploration of the diurnal to the eternal, and the continuum they span is a spirited gamble of sense enlivenings. Or, as Esteve Plantada asserts of Gual's work, "the match that sparks an idea and transforms it into [. . .] a meadow or a revelation . . .".

Profound & Excluded

Look how the grass breathes,
how hard its leaves beat
pumping plasma tinged green.

* * *

Translation is about choice, of portals before you, surrounding you. Which do you choose? Where do you go? Simply, you go. Whether it be through a doorway, however imposing; whether it be a gateway to further information, enriched emotion, enhanced resources; whether a nexus between the material and the spiritual; whether from one state of consciousness to another; venous nourishment before conveying the blood back to the heart. In fact, the process is not unlike what Gual writes in "Inner Forest"—"I'll grope along the roots/to feel the way." Key to the process for me are somatic instinct and mysterious intuition walking hand in hand with a dedicated meticulousness of an attentive mind.

From my first encounter with her work, I was drawn to Gual's dense, intense poems, and, despite Catalan being a romance language, brief on prepositional clauses, as in "Of Concentric Orbits":

> I don't fall, I throw myself.
>
> I twist my neck, swivel my elbows,
> flip trick my waist, bend my knees,
> flex my ankles,
> roll up my body.
>
> It's only a test
> to know
> if I still can, if I am living,
> if I still am.

or often, prepositional phrases serving to slow down the poem after a barrage of verbs and images. From "Needing to Make a Hole":

> I grab a shovel and a rake
> and start digging down,
> breaking the tiles first,
> smashing the cement second
> and the earth that holds it and all
> the stones I find I shove
> into my pockets in case
> of a sudden landslide

Her use of unexpected imagery to describe the speaker's state of being, feelings, or thoughts is another hallmark of her work. At times, with the more surreal poems, I only believed what I was reading when I double- or triple-checked the vocabulary. Furthermore, it may be partly Gual's audiovisual background in play, for sight is the most important sense in *Unnameable* and countless words and images evoke sight (and site), eyes (and I): see, search, seek, seem, sight, silhouette, light, bright, lightning, look; as in "Touch": "despite the eyes that shout *look*", or, "Dendrochronology": writing of the art itself!: "You're looking for a poetry . . ."

Reading and rereading, the work allows the verses' rhythms and my emotions within them to sink deep into my body. Additionally, reading over the entire collection allows me to identify key images, moods, and words sown into the whole. This will come into play later when, reviewing the new work in English, I know I can use, or reappoint, these aspects as the author has. It is a matter of understanding Catalan, of course, but also, and crucially, of apprehending Gual's own personal language within that context. For instance, the poem "Convalescence" and its final two lines:

> I swoon,
> borne by nothingness.

"Pass out" seemed too practical for someone who recently had copper wires extracted from their mouth. At the same time, does "swoon" sound archaic? It certainly resonates differently than "pass out" or "faint." I did not interpret the speaker to be unconscious, partially because, in this poem, they are conscious within the "swoon"—aware of being "borne in nothingness." And also partially because any passivity from a speaker in a Gual poem would be surprising and sound inaccurate. For me, the speaker actively feels this nothingness, this alternative reality of being in love. I chose "nothingness" instead of "void" since, though there are plenty of hollowed-out spaces or plain holes in Gual's oeuvre, they are points of discovery of content, not voids. Additionally, in her writing, she explores aspects of the pregnant body. For me, "borne" here, (and not "sustained," "buoyed," or "held") resonated well with this recurring theme of the family or network of poems in your hands.

I brought this poem to a translation workshop with these two lines as my inquiry; my plea for help. Unfortunately, the other translators did not have what I was dearly hoping for—a magic answer that simply clicked. In other words, I was still on my own. Was this to be one of those forever gnawing lines of indecision-within-decision? Was it a case of the English not having an appropriate response for the Catalan? The workshop guide, known for pushing the envelope of what is a "good" or "correct" translation, made me feel more comfortable with both my struggle and its answer-within-a-persistent-question. This was two years ago, so time and the development it allows also plays a role in the unraveling, unburdening, and enlightening of conundrums. Or not, as the case may be.

⋆ ⋆ ⋆

I translate from Catalan, French, and Spanish and am extremely grateful for the English language's contractions. I find it hard to imagine any English-language translator taking them for granted, as English speakers might. I like to consider how they can change tone, atmosphere, and pacing. With Gual's work, my first drafts contained more contractions than the final poems here. I questioned and questioned again, always also aloud, the sound of those clauses, noting that to meet Gual's condensed lyric, the contraction was an ally, and could help me achieve my goal of coming to near matches in English to Gual's short, direct—and occasionally curt—constructions.

One poem that appears here in a revised form since its publication in *Poetry*—which made Gual only the third Catalan, and the first Catalan woman, to be featured in the magazine—is "Inner Journey." On the other hand, in order to preserve moments of what I perceive as the eternal and/or mystical in Gual's work, there were times—such as in the final line of "The Evidence"—when I deliberately avoided contractions: ". . . Infinite the caress that is to come." I did this to slow the reader down, just as the feeling or fact of anticipation slows time, just as the word "caress"—its sounds and meaning in motion—slows time, just as anything infinite expands time.

Returning to Gual's blog, *I'm not falling, I am throwing myself,* that particular line, or, notably, a version of it, appears in her poem "Of Concentric Orbits": "I don't fall, I throw myself." I chose this grammatical construction to address the urgency of the situation. The blog was a regular publication, so the present continuous fits. For the poem, however, this is an occasion, and a potent one at that. The present indicative is called for, as well as, for me, the decisions to use contractions at both possible moments.

One recurring challenge in translating Gual's work is attempting to capture the tension in the original—to search for *le mot juste* for each word and line, locating potentialities then deciding on approximations of each detail while respecting the overarching image, cadence, and thematic concern. That is, by stepping back and, conversely, seeing the forest for the trees. I have set about to transmit a level of energy, of vibration, while attempting to reveal some mystery of the existential interstices to which Gual has committed herself. In the end, I am grateful for searches, as well as for my willingness to push the syntax; to have been able to follow most of her lineation, and not simply, of course, as an exercise, but as additional reverberatory, sonic, and visual rhythmic elements which might resound Gual's own musicality.

For instance, in "Reader in the Grotto," as the last line, I chose "You still don't get me," instead of "you still don't understand me," to continue a more direct, and a much less, to my ear, rambling finish, which additionally echoes the "grasping's" and "getting's" from other poems—a type of ending which I know from Gual is something she often has in mind. Certain words I've chosen—such as "phalanges," "revelation," and "aurcate" in "Maladroit," or "Twine" and "Aureate Border" elsewhere—are less typical in contemporary English-language poetry, to the point that they might risk pulling the reader out of the poem. Yet, in my experience, such words are more commonly used in Romance languages and often carry greater precision. In short, a trade-off.

In the end, I feel free in that I think of these considered and cared for versions of language and meaning to be just that: versions, interpretations, dwellings in possibilities. "Gual" means graceful and (safe!) passage, and I wish to provide a similar crossing for her poetry from her Catalan into my English. With her contemporary yet age-old sensitivity, as well as for the wonder and gravity she shares through her writing, Gual's work presents a rare literary gem to her generation, and to all of us. It is both a delightful and deeply satisfying venture to bring her unsettling poems to readers of my own mother tongue. I can hope——as Walter Benjamin writes in his essay—that I have touched upon the "imagined, inner relationship among language . . . ," this "relationship of special convergence" that can be translation.[4]

—AKaiser
Barcelona, Brooklyn 2025

4. Walter Benjamin, "The Task of the Translator," trans. Steven Rendall, *TTR: Traduction, terminologie, rédaction* 10, no. 2 (1997): 154, https://doi.org/10.7202/037302ar.

Fracassar millor

És així. Tèrbol despertar
a les històries dels altres.

Ens donen temes que hem d'omplir.
Gibrelles plenes de traves.

Quan tenim un impediment
la creació arriba.

Quan la mà escriu
es fa palès que hi ha un narrador
que pensa mentre invoca.

Error d'exercici.
Correcció de paraules.

He llegit i he entès
i he fallat,
però no en va.

Fail Better

It's like that. Murky awakening
to the stories of others.

They give us outlines we've to fill in.
Bushels full of obstacles.

Creation comes
with impediment.

When the hand writes
it becomes clear there's a narrator
who thinks while invoking.

Exercise error.
Word correction.

I've read and understood
and I've failed,
but not in vain.

INNOMBRABLE UNNAMEABLE

Pa i ceba

Les formigues recullen amb pinces
el crani de les roses.

Us esperem a la porxada
on ens balla l'ànima.

Tenim un alfabet
que ens entreté de la mort.

Bread & Onion

The ants gather with tweezers
the skulls of roses.

We'll be waiting for you on the porch
where the soul leads our dance.

We have an alphabet
to distract us from death.

D'òrbites concèntriques

No caic, em tiro.

Torço el coll, giro els colzes,
voltejo la cintura, moc els genolls,
tombo els turmells,
m'enrotllo el cos.

Només és una prova
per saber
si encara puc, si visc,
si encara sóc.

A 30° de la realitat,
elevo el cos i tallo el fil.

A 2967 m. d'altitud,
orientació nord-oest,
ja no t'enyoro.

El mal d'altura ho cura tot.

Of Concentric Orbits

I don't fall, I throw myself.

I twist my neck, swivel my elbows,
flip trick my waist, bend my knees,
flex my ankles,
roll up my body.

It's only a test
to know
if I still can, if I am living,
if I still am.

At 30° from reality,
I lift my body and cut the cord.

At an altitude of 9,734 feet,
orientation northeast,
I no longer miss you.

The fear of heights cures everything.

Teoria del caos

A la superfície
de la meva pell d'humana
hi ha restes
de saliva, petons, carícies, mossegades,
esperma,
xuclets,
talls, ferides, cops, llagues,
suor, cicatrius,
rascades, sang, crostes, blaus, lesions,
esgarrapades,
bufetades,
varius, butllofes i cremades.

No em calen ni perforacions ni tatuatges,

el meu cos
és un mapa.

Chaos Theory

On the surface
of my human skin
there are remains
of saliva, kisses, caresses, bites,
sperm,
hickeys,
cuts, wounds, blows, sores,
sweat, scars,
scratches, blood, scabs, bruises, injuries,
scrapes,
slaps,
varicose veins, blisters and burns.

No need for piercings or tattoos,

my body
is a map.

Convalescència

L'home que assegura
que m'estima
m'acosta els dits a la boca
i amb delicadesa
n'extreu fils de coure.

Surten de la gola.

Quan els acaricia
se li fonen als palmells.

Jo resto desmaiada,
sostinguda en el no-res.

Convalescence

The man who assures me
he loves me
brings his fingers to my mouth
and delicately
extracts copper wires.

They're drawn from the throat.

When he caresses them
they melt in the palms of his hands.

I swoon,
borne by nothingness.

Tan sols és fred

No et pots arribar a imaginar
la immensitat d'aquest moment:

sobre la pell m'hi he descobert
una fina capa de gel.

Pinto les ratlles dels folis
quadriculats amb tippex, tiro farina
damunt el teclat de l'ordinador,
submergeixo tota la roba
que m'omple l'armari en una galleda
amb lleixiu concentrat.

No puc esperar
a veure la neu.

It's Just Cold

You can't imagine
the immensity of this moment:

on my skin, I've discovered
a thin layer of ice.

With Wite-Out, I paint stripes
on the ruled sheets of paper, throw flour
on the keyboard,
submerge all the clothes
that fill my closet in a bucket
of concentrated lye.

I can't wait
to see the snow.

S'ha de fer forat

Agafo una pala i un rasclet
i començo a cavar cap avall,
trencant primer les rajoles,
esmicolant després el ciment
i la terra que el sosté i totes
les pedres que trobo les deso
a les butxaques per si
tot d'una visc una esllavissada
i cal fer un mur i esperar
que la cosa es calmi.

No vull pensar
on arribaré ni quan tardaré
ni si al final hi trobaré
algú cavant en sentit contrari.

Qui sap si xocaré,
sense tenir temps
per prevenir la col·lisió,
contra el cap d'algú
ple de fang i runa.

La veritat, pànic de xocar
contra mi,
de ser jo la pregunta i la resposta.

Needing to Make a Hole

I grab a shovel and a rake
and start digging down,
breaking the tiles first,
smashing the cement second
and the earth that holds it and all
the stones I find I shove
into my pockets in case
of a sudden landslide
and I'd have to throw a wall up and wait
for things to calm down.

I don't want to think
about where I'm headed or how long it'll take,
or if in the end I'll find
someone digging in the opposite direction.

Who knows if I'll smash,
with no time
to prevent the collision,
against someone's head
full of mud and rubble.

Truth is, panic to crash
into myself,
to be myself the question and the answer.

Viatge interior

No ho diguis a ningú:
m'he empassat la pedra
que m'ha fet caure
he alçat el cos
aprofitant un cop de vent.

Si em moc és
gràcies al dolor que em llisca
esòfag avall,
fetge avall, estómac avall,
intestí gros avall,
abdomen avall, genolls avall,
víscera endins.

Que per què escric?
Perquè no sé parlar ni en vull aprendre.

Inner Journey

Don't tell anyone:
I swallowed the stone
that made me fall
and I've lifted my body up
taking advantage of a gust of wind.

If I move it's
thanks to the pain that slips
down my esophagus,
to my liver below, stomach below,
large intestine below,
abdomen below, knees below,
viscera inside.

Why do I write?
Because I don't know how to speak and I don't want to learn.

Escorça

Frases com «a recer guanyo
el combat»,
«els secrets a l'espai perden el so»
o «retalls de pell
avançant pel passadís»
me les guardo per mi.

També emmagatzemo paraules:

abisme, subsòl, saliva, paràsit,
trencadissa,
mudesa,
lentament,
impacte, latitud,
etern,
amarg,
invisible, hivern, profunditat, ferida, túnel.

Sóc portadora de significat.

I no el trec.

Crust

Phrases like "by seeking shelter, I win
the fight,"
"secrets in space lose their sound"
or "skin scraps
making their way down the hallway"
I keep for myself.

I also store words like:

abyss, underground, saliva, parasite,
brittle,
mute,
slowly,
impact, latitude,
eternal,
bitter,
invisible, winter, depth, wound, tunnel.

I'm a bearer of meaning.

And it's beyond my reach.

Pendís

Corro per la nit.

Cap ull entre la boira,
cap soroll estrany, cap ressò de crit.

Corro per la nit,
travessant la nit, untant-me de foscor.

Travesso la nit, travesso el desert,
travesso la por dels que dormiu.

Corro per la nit,
em crec nit,
sóc el mort del carreró.

Penetro la nit i la nit em penetra a mi.

Em corro dins la nit.

Faig el vagabund,
faig de prostíbul ambulant,
tremolo
de cuixes i d'esperit.

Corro per la nit.

Cap ull entre la boira,
cap soroll estrany, cap ressò de crit.

Descent

I run in the night.

No eye amid the mist,
No strange noise, no echo of a cry.

I run in the night,
traversing the night, anointing me with shadow.

I cross the night, cross the desert,
cross the fear of those who sleep.

I run in the night,
I believe I am night,
I'm alleyway death.

I penetrate the night and the night penetrates me.

I run inside the night.

I play the vagabond,
I play the wandering prostitute,
quiver
in my thighs and soul.

I run in the night.

No eye amid the mist,
no strange noise, no echo of a cry.

No és la nit
la que m'espanta
sinó el xiscle estrangulat
que em puja pel pit.

Podria ser pitjor:
La nit es corre
dins de mi,
la nit escup baba blanca
en un racó ombrívol
d'un úter fonedís.

It isn't the night
that frightens me
but the strangling scream
that climbs up my chest.

It could be worse:
The night runs
inside of me,
the night spits white phlegm
in the dim corner
of a molten womb.

Innombrable

Deixa que entri el gos
a ensumar les misèries de la casa.

Que bordi quan olori l'olor gastada
de la roba,
que bordi quan localitzi cabells blancs
flotant per l'aire,
que bordi quan la pols que ronda
les cambres mortes
li enteli la vista i li dificulti els passos,
que bordi quan detecti endolls
precintats
i làmpades amb bombetes foses,
que bordi quan topi amb la memòria,
quan trepitgi
la rajola que amaga un feix de rostres,
que bordi i que s'espanti
quan escolti
les corredisses dels espectres,
quan trobi ombres adherides
a les parets
i crits enganxats al sostre,
que bordi quan s'apropi a la tomba
on dorm la pena
i que calli de cop
i es deixi emportar
quan la pena es desperti
i l'arrossegui.

Unnameable

Let the dog in
to sniff the house's miseries.

Let him bark when he smells the worn smell
of the clothes,
let him bark when he finds white hair
floating through the air,
let him bark when the dust wandering about
the dead chambers
clouds his vision and trips him up,
let him bark when he senses sockets
sealed
and lamps with molten bulbs,
let him bark when he bumps into memory
when he steps on
tile hiding an array of faces,
let him bark and be spooked
when he hears
ghosts gliding,
when he finds shadows hewed
to the walls
and screams glued to the ceiling,
let him bark when he nears the grave
where sorrow sleeps
when suddenly he'll go quiet
and let himself be taken
when pain wakes
and drags him away.

Excavacions

Els meus forats són tres
i mal proporcionats.

El meu, el vostre i el de ningú.

El que omplo jo fa
        2,9 cm. de diàmetre per
        3,2 cm. de profunditat
i està ple de boles de neu.

El que omplo amb tot allò
que es troba a l'exterior
        té un radi de 17 mm.,
        la seva profunditat en fa 13
i acull camins de pedres
i marges feréstecs
on hi reposen fulles seques.

El tercer, el de ningú,
        fa 5,9 cm. de diàmetre
        per 7,4 de profunditat
i resta buit.

Tot i tenir la certesa
que mai s'omplirà,
és el que més estimo.

Excavations

My own holes number three
and are ill-proportioned.

Mine, yours and nobody's.

The one that I fill measures
    1.1 inches in diameter by
    1.2 inches in depth
and is full of snowballs.

The one I fill with all that
located on the outside
    has a radius of .6 inches,
    its depth measures .5 inches
and it holds stone paths
and wild banks
where dry leaves lie.

The third, that of nobody's,
    measures 2.3 inches in diameter
    by 2.9 inches in depth
and remains empty.

Despite the certainty
that it will never be filled,
it's the one I love most.

Hipertensió

La pressió
sempre ha estat elevada
al nivell en què em moc.

Perquè si no arrisco no visc
i si no visc no té sentit escriure
i com viure sense escriure?

Així que la pressió
sempre ha estat elevada
al nivell en què em moc,
perquè vull escriure, i no hi ha escrit sincer
sense que el cap del que escriu
exploti.

i per això tot el que faig
és a pressió i porta problemes,
perquè els problemes
són moviment, són lluita, són motor.

I per això tot el que faig
és a pressió i porta problemes,
perquè els problemes són inspiració.

I el viure surant
que se'l quedi un altre, que jo vull
menjar
terrossos de terra.

Hypertension

At the level I move
    pressure
    has always been high.

Because if I don't risk I don't live
and if I don't live, there's no sense in writing
and how to live without writing?

So at the level I move
    pressure
    has always been high
because I want to write, and there's no true writing
unless the head of the writer
                                        explodes.

This is why everything I do
is under pressure and causes problems
because the problems
are movement, are struggle, are engine.

And this is why everything I do
is under pressure and causes problems
because the problems are inspiration.

A floating life
is another life, while I want
to eat
clods of earth.

I la cuirassa transparent
que la vesteixi un altre, que jo vull
enganxar-me
els dits a cada porta,
que jo vull entrar a un tornado i donar voltes
i tirar-me a un riu cabalós
i que se m'emporti.

La probabilitat de quedar-m'hi
            sempre ha estat elevada
            al nivell en què em moc,
perquè si vull escriure he de viure i no patir
per si se'm para
                el cor.

And the transparent armor
dresses another, while I want
to stick
my fingers into every door hinge,
while I want to jump into a tornado and spin
and throw myself into a raging river
and let it take me away.

Chances I'll stay like this
    the pressure always high
    at the level I move
because if I want to write I need to live and not suffer
just because my heart might
                stop.

Commoció

Se cerró el sol, se cerró el sentido del sol,
se iluminó el sentido de cerrarse.
—Alejandra Pizarnik

El record d'unes ungles
amb escates de llum el tinc
present sovint. També
porto amb mi un pantà ple
d'estrelles, l'ombra
d'un bosc sencer cremant,
les espurnes d'un toll de lava
i una desena de rostres
avançant entre la boira
a la llum brillant dels llamps.

En la memòria d'un cec un raig
de sol s'incrusta en un vidre entelat.

Commotion

The sun shut down, the meaning of the sun shut down,
the meaning of shutting down lit up.
—Alejandra Pizarnik

The memory of some fingernails
scaled in light is often present
in my mind. Also
I carry in me a swamp full
of stars, the shadow
of an entire forest ablaze,
sparks from a pool of lava
and a dozen faces
advancing through the fog
lit by bright lightning.

In the memory of a blind person a ray
of sun embedded in a clouded glass.

Renec

Jo no volia un mapa.
Jo volia un matxet per obrir-me pas
a la selva, seguint l'inconscient.

Quan diuen *massa tard*,
vols dir que potser no exageren?

He trobat un petit ganivet
i crec que podré tallar les plantes
que se'm fiquen als ulls,
les que m'obstrueixen la voluntat,
les que exalten les contradiccions.

Sí,
jo no volia un mapa.

Jo volia un Déu dins de cadascú.

Profanity

I didn't want a map.
I wanted a machete to clear a path
in the jungle, to follow the unconscious.

When they say *too late*,
you mean maybe they're not exaggerating?

I found a small knife
and I think I'll be able to cut the plants
that get into my eyes,
those that obstruct my will,
those that glorify contradictions.

That's right,
I didn't want a map.

I wanted a God within everyone.

Granulat

Oblidar què és un rellotge.
No reconèixer l'instrument.

Intuir que el temps és el breu balanceig
d'una barca amarrada a un port mil·lenari.

Ser la boia,
ser el fons marí,
ser el rovell de l'àncora.

Conviccions que no són d'ara.

Granulated

Forget what a watch is.
Don't recognize the instrument.

Intuit that time is the brief swing
of a boat moored in a millennial port.

Be the buoy,
be the seabed,
be the rust of the anchor.

Convictions not of our now.

Transhumància mental

Es mentem només
les coses palpables.

Jo crec en allò que no veig.
Si ho veig, desconfio.

Se'm malmet el pensament
si puc tocar allò que és dit.

L'invisible
ens guarirà.

Mental Transhumance

We mention only
palpable things.

I believe in what I don't see.
If I see it, I'm suspicious.

The thought is spoiled
if I can touch what's said.

The invisible
will heal us.

Mil·límetres

No passa res, no passa res.

Els camins no porten enlloc
però no és greu,

tampoc en sabem res del desert
i bé que hi anem i el fotografiem
i fem com qui el reconeix
                                        i l'entén.

Avui comença alguna cosa.

I sempre que comença alguna
cosa és perquè abans n'ha mort
una altra per deixar-li espai.

Millimeters

Nothing's happening. Nothing is happening.

Paths lead nowhere
but no matter,

nor do we know anything of the desert
even if we go there and take photos
and go about as if we recognize
                                        and understand it.

Today something is beginning.

And always, if something's beginning
it's because something else died before
to leave space for it.

Estepa

Has mudat en danses els meus planys,
m'has tret el dol i m'has vestit de festa.
Salm 30:11

Quan es fa fosc
entren els llangardaixos
i tot és per tu.

Entren les serps
i tot és per tu.

De matinada entren els trons,
m'entren els llamps
i és per tu
que ja no temo els animals
ni el raig de sol
que em travessa el pit.

Estepa, Hypericum Balearicum

You've transformed my sorrow into dance,
You've undressed my mourning and draped me with joy.
Psalm 30:11

When night falls
the lizards come in
and it's all your doing.

The snakes come in
and it's all your doing.

At dawn thunder claps,
lightning strikes me
and it's your doing
that I no longer fear animals
nor the ray of sun
that pierces my chest.

Magma

Una pedra es desplaça silenciosa
uns nanòmetres al llarg d'un segle
i no en sabem res.

Conversen els fetus entre ells
i ni ens n'adonem.

La necessitat de trobar un adjectiu
entre *visible* i *invisible*.

Magma

A stone moves silently
a few nanometers a century
and we know nothing about it.

Fetuses talk to each other
and we don't even register it.

The need to find an adjective
between *visible* and *invisible*.

Brots

Entre lletra i lletra
hi neix un munt d'herba
que no penso tallar.

He tornat a desenterrar significats,
a tensar les paraules ajuntant-les.

Mira'm com contemplo,
com em cruix el cos
només en l'acte de mirar.

Estirar les definicions
com qui estira els ossos
en el moment de llevar-se.

Allargar els sons
perquè t'arribin les ones
ara que ets totes les cases,
tots els rebosts,
tots els refugis nuclears.

Deixa de repetir en veu baixa
que no em vols al costat del llit
si escric així, que et sento.

Les coses no són el que semblen ser,
sinó tota la resta.

Sprouts

In between letter and letter
so much grass is born
which I won't mow down.

I've returned to digging up meanings,
to tauten words by joining them.

Look how I contemplate,
how my body creaks
in the simple act of looking.

Stretch definitions
as one who stretches her muscles
as she gets up.

Lengthen sounds
so the waves reach you
now that you're all the houses,
all the pantries,
all the nuclear shelters.

Stop repeating in a low voice
that you don't want me next to the bed
if I write like this, I hear you.

Things are not as they seem,
but all the rest.

Efectes

No és a la nit sinó al capvespre,
a l'hora blava, quan deu mil ocells
a la renglera d'un cable elèctric
es posen d'acord i aguanten l'alè,
apreten les ales i se'ls dispara
el batec, la sang de les potes els bull
i calculen quants nusos té el vent,
com si fos el primer cop, com si fos
el darrer, i es repeteixen per dins
som
a punt
a punt
a punt
de travessar el cel i creuar el continent.

La força de l'impuls
reverbera el fil elèctric,
fa baixar
per uns segons
la intensitat
de les bombetes.

Ningú
entén el perquè.

Effects

It's not at night but at dusk,
the blue hour, when ten thousand birds
in a row on an electric wire
come to an agreement and hold their breath,
spread their wings and beating hearts
cocked, blood in legs boiling
calculate how many knots there are in the wind,
as if for the first time, as if
for the last, and repeat among themselves
we are
set
set
set
to cross the sky and traverse the continent.

The force of the impulse
reverberates along the wire,
lessens
for a few seconds
the intensity
of light bulbs.

No one
understands why.

Selva interior

Crec que m'he desviat de l'asfalt.
Crec que això que em fereix són branques.

Sé que no he de posar-me severa
però el bosc s'està espessint i tampoc
caldria fer veure que no m'espanta.

A les fosques la boira no apareix.
A les fosques no ressona quan m'abraço.

Palparé les arrels
per sentir el camí.

Si trobo nèctar i un niu amb larves
potser encara hi haurà esperança.

Quanta innocència s'amaga
entre els arbres
que em volen acollir a la fageda.

Quanta tardor aplegada
als genolls tous d'aquesta natura morta,
d'aquest pou,
d'aquest mur que diu que es trenca,
que s'esquerda per les venes.

Inner Forest

I think I've veered from the pavement.
I think what hurts me are the branches.

I know I shouldn't take it all too seriously
but the forest is thickening and I don't
have to pretend it doesn't scare me.

In the dark, fog is unseen.
In the dark, there's no resonance when I hold myself.

I'll grope along the roots
to feel the way.

If I find nectar and a nest of larvae
there may still be hope.

How much innocence hides
among the trees
as they welcome me to the beech forest.

How much autumn gathers
on soft knees all of this still life,
this well,
this wall that says it's breaking,
that it's cracking along its veins.

No em trobaràs quan les coses
prenguin el nom de la tristesa.

No em trobaràs
perquè estaré al revers
de les paraules.

You won’t find me when things
take on the name of sadness.

You won’t find me
because I’ll be on the other side
of words.

T'estimem per qui no ets

No es pot ésser exescriptor
com no es pot ésser exalcohòlic.

La condició rau a dins.

We Love You for Who You're Not

You can't be an ex-writer
like you can't be an ex-alcoholic.

The condition lies within.

Sobirania

Les coses petites necessiten parella.

Dos ulls.
Dues orelles.
Dos braços.
Dos turmells.
Dos colzes.
Dues mans.
Dos mugrons.
Dues cames.
Dos ovaris.
Dos testicles.
Dos genolls.
Dos peus.

Però la mort, la mort és tan gran
que només n'hi pot haver una.

Sovereignty

Little things need their partner.

Two eyes.
Two ears.
Two arms.
Two ankles.
Two elbows.
Two hands.
Two nipples.
Two legs.
Two ovaries.
Two testicles.
Two knees.
Two feet.

But death, death is so great
there can only be one.

L'evidència

Un vestit estampat amb algues
o unes algues damunt d'un cos
convertides en vestit, o millor,
una pell camuflada entre algues,
això, una pell camuflada entre
algues dins del mar tèrbol, no,
surant, surant damunt l'oceà,
no, surant, surant damunt d'un
riu, això, surant, baixant el corrent
riu transparent cap avall, això,
riu transparent fluint cap endins.

Flota a l'aire un desconegut misteri.

Infinita la carícia que ha de venir.

The Evidence

A seaweed print dress
or some algae on a body
turned into a dress, or better,
a skin camouflaged among algae,
yes, that, a skin camouflaged among
algae inside the sea, blooming, no,
floating, floating on the ocean,
no, floating, floating on a
river, that's it, floating downstream
transparent river downward, yes, that,
transparent river flowing inward.

Unknown mystery hanging in the air.

Infinite the caress that is to come.

Judici

Horitzontal, fila 12:
Obstacle a sortejar en plena autopista
          (tres lletres, acabat en n),
hi he posat "ren"
i al final el que quadrava era "con".

Si segueixo anant contra direcció
em tatuaré amb bolígraf permanent
un relat autobiogràfic al ventre
per no haver de respondre mai més
          d'on vinc,
                    què he viscut,
                    com m'han enganyat,
          a qui he fet mal,
     per què he patit,
                              quant
                              he perdut.

Tot per acabar dient que el que un aprèn,
amb el pas dels anys, és a no fer preguntes.

Judgment

Horizontal, row 12:
Obstacle that might be seen in the middle of the highway
(four letters, ending in e),
I put "adoe"
and in the end what worked was "cone."

If I keep going in the opposite direction
I'll tattoo myself with a sharpie
an autobiographical tale on the belly
to never have to answer again
where I come from
what I've lived
how I've been deceived,
who I've hurt
why I've suffered
how much
I've lost.

All of this, in the end, is to say that what you learn,
over the years, is to not ask questions.

Autoconscient

Escric com escric perquè
sóc animal abans que persona
i persona abans que poeta.

I amb viure el mateix, però més dolorós.

Self-Conscious

I write as I write because
I am an animal before person
and person before poet.

And to live this, but more painfully.

Aliatge de coure i níquel

Les coses existeixen
per ser trencades.

Prendre'n consciència asserena.

Copper & Nickel Alloy

Things exist
to be broken.

To realize it, serene.

Adults

Comptabilitzats:

51 secrets incrustats a les taquetes
microscòpiques de les pupil·les,
8 decepcions surant a la superfície
remoguda de la glàndula llagrimal,
14 mentides retingudes a la capa
rugosa de la llengua, amb la saliva,
27 pecats amagats a la penombra
que habita la intersecció de la carn.

Som la brutalitat del bastó
d'un cec que pel passeig es troba
un altre cec, i el fa caure.

Adults

Accounted for:

51 secrets embedded in the microscopic
stains of the pupils,
8 disappointments floating on the surface
removed from the lacrimal gland,
14 lies kept in the rough cloak
of the tongue, along with saliva,
27 sins hidden in the shadows
that inhabit the crossways of the flesh.

We are the brutality of the cane
of a blind person who runs into
another, and makes them fall.

Maldestres

Riem perquè no sabem barallar-nos.
Riem perquè encara
no hem après
a interpretar els nostres presagis.

A les parets de les cèl·lules s'hi enganxa
l'etern.
Però no hi entra.

Quan el pintor hagi acabat
el nostre retrat
serem esquelets units per les falanges:

finestres de calç cercant sempre
la mateixa pregunta.

Maladroit

We laugh because we don't know how to fight.
We laugh because still
we haven't learned
to interpret our omens.

The eternal
sticks to cell walls.
But doesn't enter.

When the painter has finished
our portrait
we'll be skeletons united by the phalanges:

lime windows forever searching for
the same question.

Re-re-re-besàvia

El dret a rendir-nos no és un dret,
deuries dir a algú que se m'assemblava.
És un error semàntic.
És un engany de magma.

Tots els segles són el mateix segle.
Només canvien els colors i les formes.
Els costums.
Els bacteris.

Tu sempre has habitat tots els temps.
Sempre m'has viscut a dins.
Viva i morta, a la vegada.

Amb l'ànim de qui empeny,
descalça,
un carruatge.

Great-Great-Great-Great Grandmother

The right to surrender is not a right,
you should tell someone who resembled me.
It's a semantic error.
It's a magma hoax.

All centuries are the same century.
Only the colors and shapes change.
The customs.
The bacteria.

You have always inhabited all times.
You have always lived inside me.
Alive and dead, at the same time.

Urged on by those who push,
barefoot,
a carriage.

Licor d'ullastre

La mà
de la meva àvia s'obre igual
que la mà d'un nadó.

Tant de misteri
bloqueja tota la maldat
que hagi de venir.

Wild Olive Spirits

The hand
of my grandmother opens like
the hand of a baby.

So much mystery
blocks all the evil
that must come.

L'ocult natural

Han estat moments increïbles, aquests.

He vist morir un home
i he vist matar-ne
d'un cop sec un altre.

N'he vist plorar a sanglots
uns quants, n'he vist bastants
que al carrer sagnaven.

Si torno és perquè necessito
contemplar en primera persona
un naixement.

Poder notar a flor de pell
com un forat escup un cos
i dels grumolls en surt un ser
amb dos micropulmons
i dues minicames.

Saber que passarà els dies
respirant i desplaçant-se, movent-se,
cercant en va
una llista de coses estables.

Però no dir-li res.
Callar-li l'esventada.

The Natural Occult

Some incredible moments these have been.

I have seen a man die
and I have seen one kill another
with one blow.

I've seen some sob
and many others
bleed in the streets.

If I go back it's because I need
to contemplate in the first person
a birth.

To sense with a shiver
how a hole spits out a body
and from lumps comes a being
with two micro-lungs
and two mini-legs.

To know she'll spend days
breathing and repositioning, moving,
searching in vain
a list of stable things.

But say nothing to her.
Hush the chatter.

Silenciar el vent huracanat,
la força del corrent,
els terratrèmols,
els diluvis, les sotragades.

Somriure al fill,
prémer fort la mà de la mare.

Silence the hurricane wind,
the force of the current,
the earthquakes,
the floods, the shocks.

Smile at the child,
squeeze hard the mother's hand.

Lector a la gruta

Pobre aquell que repetirà el procés
de l'abandó. Pobre aquell per ser-ne l'amo.

Si em vaig fullejant els llavis
em llegeixo les entranyes
com si fos un profeta amagat
rere la porta
que m'ha de conduir
a l'ànima.

Vaig néixer cova.
Encara no m'heu entès.

Reader in the Grotto

Poor thing who'll repeat the process
of abandonment. Poor thing for being the master.

If I leaf through my lips
I read my guts
as if I were a hidden prophet
behind the door
that has to lead me
to the soul.

I was born a cave.
You still don't get me.

Cordills

Al darrere de la cuirassa
hi amagues una capa d'atzar
que encercla la revelació
que et veurà enlairar-te.

Venja't, si cal, de la història que t'expliquen
i de les ales del mite
que t'ha de brotar entre els omòplats.

La tinta que regalimes als contorns,
és de marbre o és d'abisme?

Seguiré esperant que el poema respongui,
tot i que sé que el poema no respon mai.

Twine

Behind the suit of armor
hides a layer of chance
encircling the revelation
that will see you soar.

Take revenge, if necessary, for the story they tell you
and from the wings of the myth
that should sprout between your shoulder blades.

The ink that seeps at the margins,
is it marble or abyss?

I will keep waiting for the poem to respond,
though I know the poem never responds.

Profund i exclòs

Mira com respire l'herba,
com de fort li batega la tija
bombejant plasma verdós.

Coordenades d'una zona
de brillantors intravenoses
i els llençols enganxats
a l'orella del son ardent.

Ets del revés,
giravoltant la matèria
que sosté el temps de cera.

Per què vas anar a dormir sense mirar-te les mans?
Qui et traurà ara la sang lletosa de la comissura?

La corona de flors és al terrat,
per si se t'acut tenyir les plantes.

Profound & Excluded

Look how the grass breathes,
how hard its leaves beat
pumping plasma tinged green.

Coordinates of an area
of intravenous glint
and sheets stuck
to the ear of burning sleep.

You're upside down
twirling the matter
sustaining wax time.

Why did you go to sleep without looking at your hands?
Who will clean the milky blood from your corner now?

The crown of flowers is on the rooftop,
in case you're thinking of dyeing the plants.

Tàctil

Tons verds el perseguien
quan baixava per les escales.

L'aliança del moribund salvatge
amb els seus fills urbans
no va ser plàcida.
Tampoc sincera.

Una disfressa coberta
amb dues condicions:

Fils daurats
per cosir els traus dels sacs de dormir.

Fils d'espart
per relligar el llibre dels vicis.

Tactile

Shades of green chased him
as he descended the stairs.

The Covenant of the Dying Savage
with her urban children
was not smooth
nor sincere.

A costume covered
under two conditions:

Golden threads
to sew the eyelets of the sleeping bags.

Esparto grasses
to tie up the book of vices.

Terrabastall

Es tracta, en primer lloc,
de fer una perforació.
Tant se val la mida.

Es tracta, més endavant,
de rectificar l'obertura.
D'empetitir-la o de fer-la més gran.
D'adaptar-la als prodigis
que la mandíbula s'inventa.

Es tracta, sobretot,
de crear un espai buit
on guardar-hi allò que cou,
allò que s'extravia.

Cal adaptar l'avenc a la dimensió
de cada instant.

Constrènyer la proesa.

Racket

It's about, first of all,
making a hole.
Size doesn't matter.

It's about, later,
rectifying the opening.
To make it smaller or larger.
To adapt it to the prodigies
the jaw has invented.

It is, above all,
to create an empty space
where to store what evaporates,
what gets lost.

You have to adapt the chasm to the dimension
of every moment.

Constrict the capacity.

Abundància

Si la poesia és un animal,
serà un animal
que fugi per totes bandes.

Trepitjant-se les urpes
a cada pas, a la recerca d'ell mateix,
inaugurant una escapade pròpia.

Rastre veloç
que trenca la nit
dels astres hiemals.

Ferida oberta
sense possibilitat de cicatriu.

Abundance

If poetry is an animal,
it will be an animal
that flees to everywhere.

Clutching its claws
at every step, in search of itself,
launching an escapade of its own.

Flash track
that shatters the night
of hiemal stars.

Open wound
no possibility of scars.

Tacte

Vèncer la claror amb més llum
i alletar la ment amb el pit de vidre
que s'esberla amb el temporal
que tot ho mou, que tot ho sacseja,
que fa vessar dies en blanc
per un esglai que diu que es queda,
que té facilitat per obrir parets de marbre,
ser de marbre i reencarnar-se en la destral
que odia el marbre:
tot en un, tot junt, tot ben junt,
perquè quan bull la llet amb fel
en queda un tel que ens dignifica
i que recorda que tots som cecs
malgrat els ulls que criden *mira*,
perquè aquest embrió que duc a dins
és més viu que tots nosaltres
i poc hi veu,
i poc hi sent,
però és tan viu que m'ennuega.

Touch

To defeat clarity with more light
and nurse the mind with the breast of glass
that shatters with the storm
that moves everything, that shakes it all,
that spills days in white
for a fright that says it's staying,
that has a talent for opening walls of marble,
being of marble and reincarnating as the ax
that detests marble:
all in one, all together, all closely together,
because when milk boils bitter
there remains a layer that dignifies
and reminds us that we are all blind
despite the eyes that shout *look*,
because this embryo that I carry inside
is more alive than all of us
and sees little,
and feels little,
but is so alive it strangles me.

Crom

Si la solidesa no existeix,
com és que l'esquelet s'aguanta?

Si el cervell és tan malparit,
com és que el coll encara el subjecta?

Carn, que vol dir descens, que vol dir
vèncer les misèries, que vol dir entaforar-se
dins les venes d'un mateix
i clavar-hi la bandera.

Començar el vers pel final.
Recomençar.
Avantnéixer.

He dit avantnéixer.
Calia dir postmorir.
Calia dir pensar cap endarrere.

Voldria perdre'm pel carreró
on es conreen els fetus.

Aquest és l'objectiu primer.
Aquesta és la meva resistència.

Chrome

If solidity does not exist,
how does a skeleton hold up?

If the brain is so wicked,
how does the neck go on supporting it?

Flesh, which means degradation,which means
overcoming misery, which means burrow
inside those veins
and nail a flag there.

Begin the verse at the end.
Begin again.
Before-birth.

I said before-birth.
I should've said post-death.
I should've said think backwards.

I'd like to get lost in the alley
where fetuses are cultivated.

This is the primary objective.
This is my resistance.

Límit herbaci

He conegut els falsos profetes
i n'he tingut por. He fugit d'ells
travessant els camps més foscos
i sé que en tornaré sencera.

Diria que ningú ha traçat aquest camí.

Diria que les fruites silvestres
que trobo són comestibles.

La immortalitat deu ser
creure's allò que un pensa
i fer-ne religió.

La immortalitat deu ser
no dur motxilla.

Hi ha animals petits
que s'escapoleixen quan m'hi apropo,
però l'animal petit que duc a dins
ve amb mi.

Ni un bri de culpa
per no haver-vos advertit
que seguia els mapes estel·lars.

Aureate Border

I've known false prophets
and they scared me. I ran away
crossing the darkest fields
and I know I'll return whole.

I'd say no one has charted this path.

I'd say the forest berries
I find are edible.

Immortality must be
to believe what you think
and make of it a religion.

Immortality must be
not to carry a backpack.

There are small animals
that run away as I approach,
but the little animal I carry inside
comes with me.

Not a shred of guilt
for not having warned you
I was following star maps.

Ni un bocí de penediment
per pensar que alletaré
la criatura com em doni la gana
i que li explicaré els contes
que vosaltres calleu.

No recordo gaires coses de l'altra vida.
Volia germinar i, allà, no podia.

El blat que els meus ulls seguen
serà el més daurat del món.

Not a bit of remorse
to think I will breastfeed
the creature as I please
and tell them tales
you silence.

I don't remember much about that other life.
I wanted to germinate and, there, I couldn't.

The wheat my eyes follow
will be the most golden in the world.

Estructures

Quin miracle,
quan una persona
segueix el patró
d'un altre cos.

Quan en té la retirada exacta.

Quina meravella,
la de les similituds intercontinentals,
la dels semblants que dialoguen
a cent mil quilòmetres transatlàntics.

La dels desconeguts
que són mirall.

Però per què ens sorprenen tant
els trets compartits
si venim tots
d'allà mateix?

Si som els clons del mateix clon.
Si som el motlle primer.

Si som un de sol.

Structures

What a miracle,
when one person
follows the pattern
of another body.

When there's an exact resemblance.

What a wonder,
that of international similarities,
of those alike in dialogue
at a distance of 100,000 transatlantic miles.

Those of strangers
mirroring each other.

But why are we so surprised by
shared traits
if we all come from
the same place?

If we're clones of the same clone.
If we're the first mold.

If we're one.

Calci i fòsfor

Combat la fugida
amb el bressol.

Diu: *aquest cos està fet per desfer-se.*

Aïllament i sordesa voluntària.
Teixit esponjós
de la ment durant l'atac.

Les cames s'escapen
de l'estructura òssia
del fetus mentre canten:
aquest cos està fet per desfer-se,
aquest cos està destinat a desaparèixer,
aquesta carn no sabrà deixar marca.

Tu no les escoltes.
Tu t'emmuralles.

Trencadís per les ossades
predecessores que retornen i clamen:
Els ossos no són peces mortes.
Els ossos estan més vius
que tots nosaltres.

I tu que t'imagines com deuen ser
les carícies d'una mare sordmuda.

I tu que t'imagines
que ets ella.

Calcium & Phosphorus

Fight flight
with the cradle.

It is said: *this body is made to be undone.*

Isolation and voluntary deafness.
Spongy tissue
of the mind during the attack.

Legs slip away
from the bone structure
of the fetus while they sing:
this body is made to be undone,
this body is destined to disappear,
this flesh won't know how to leave its mark.

You don't listen to them.
You wall yourself in.

Broken by previous bones
who return and cry out:
Bones are not dead things.
Bones are more alive
than all of us.

And you who imagine how they must be,
the caresses of a deaf-mute mother.

And you who imagine
you are her.

La cal·ligrafia oculta

Em quedaré cega
de tant mirar.

Coixa de tant repetir
la naturalesa dels trencalls.

Ja sense mans
de tant aguantar el llapis,
de tant colpejar
massa fort les pedres
entre elles,

seguiré creant
amb el crani.

Concealed Calligraphy

I'll end up sightless
from so much looking.

Lame from repeating so often
the nature of forks in the road.

Without hands now
from so holding the pencil,
from so hitting
stones too hard
against each other,

I'll keep creating
with the skull.

Holística

La humanitat és vulnerable.

El que no ho és
és l'energia prehistòrica
que ens ha dut
fins l'ara.

Connectats a través dels narius,
respirem ínfimes partícules
del mateix argó
que van respirar
fa seixanta-sis milions d'anys
els dinosaures.

Desconeixent el com,
la història ens va escrivint
mentre ens esborra.

Holistic

Humanity is vulnerable.

What's not
is the prehistoric energy
that's conducted us
till now.

Connected through the nostrils,
we breathe infinitesimal particles
of the same argon
they breathed 66 million years ago.
The dinosaurs.

Not knowing how,
history is writing us
as it erases us.

Mapa emocionat

L'inventor
el primer laberint
no va inventar res.

Sols va intentar
copier la forma divina
del seu cervell
damunt del paisatge.

Emotional Map

The inventor
of the first labyrinth
invented nothing.

They only tried
to copy the divine form
of their brain
onto the landscape.

Dendrocronologia

Escolta, el vermell no és de ningú.

La llum se l'atribueix però no és seu,
com tampoc ho és l'hort
on es congrien les energies.

Per què vols operar-te
si ja t'estima l'home de les penombres?

Tu busca una poesia
que pugui ser desxifrada
com un coneixement científic,
com un missatge
pels que vindran
d'aquí a tres segles.

No t'estressis.
La podridura no ha après
a donar la mà.

Ara bé,
un gos mort té la silueta d'una persona.

Dendrochronology

Listen, red belongs to no one.

The light is attributed to it but doesn't belong to it,
neither does the garden
where energies converge.

Why do you want to have surgery
if the man of the shadows already loves you?

You're looking for a poetry
that can be deciphered
as scientific knowledge,
as a message
for those who'll come
three centuries from now.

Don't stress over it.
Rot hasn't learned
to shake hands.

That said,
a dead dog has the silhouette of a person.

Ara sí

No ho hem d'il·luminar tot.
No cal.

Tampoc hauria de ser dit, aquest llibre.
Només viscut.

Un llibre a mitges.
Un nadó sobrevivent.

Vam néixer amb ell.

Ara l'expliquem
en veu alta.

Tot el que escrivim
és sempre
una resposta
a una pregunta no formulada.

Now, Yes

We don't have to illuminate everything.
No need.

Nor should this book be told.
It simply lived.

A half-written book.
A surviving baby.

We were born with it.

Now let's explain it
out loud.

Everything we write
is always
an answer
to an unasked question.

Sant'eustachio

El darrer so que sentiré quan mori

serà el crit que vaig fer al néixer.

Sant'Eustachio

The last sound I'll hear when I die

will be the cry I made at birth.

Cactus de sal

D'oxigen,
els textos en van plens.

Però qui els respira?
Qui els uneix?

Si escric trenco el tel que els folra.
S'incinera el seu rastre corpori.
I és alhora quan escric que recupero
la forma del mot.

Pelegrinatge al centre del dir.
Romeria al melic de l'amant.

Cada paraula és una persona.

Salt Cactus

Texts are bursting
with oxygen.

But who breathes them?
Who unites them?

If I write, I tear away at their lining.
Their bodily traces are incinerated.
And, at the same time, it's when I write I recover
the form of the word.

Pilgrimage to the center of saying.
Procession to the lover's navel.

Each word is a person.

Oracle

Tornar al poema
com tornar al pa
amb una fam primària.

Talment menjar
no per gana
sinó per voler seguir existint.

Oracle

Returning to the poem
like returning to bread
with a primary hunger.

So to eat
not from hunger
but from want to go on existing.

Meconi

En secret
el cercle té escaires, arestes
i formes quadrades.

Si et fa creure
que és un punt perfecte
és l'engany
el que et parla.

Percep la textura del peix
i ara vés
i narra-la.
Veuràs que la mentida segueix,
en aquest cas
la de la paraula
prohibida.

No hi ha alè que descrigui
el deliri viscós que silencies.

He vingut
per mirar-te l'enigma.

Fuig de tots.

No hi haurà bon port
on hi puguis amarrar la cavitat.

Meconium

In secret
the circle has angles, edges
and square shapes.

If it makes you believe
that it's a perfect point
it's deception
who's talking.

Perceive the texture of the fish
now go
recount it.
You'll see the lie continues,
in this case,
the lie of the forbidden
word.

There's no breath that describes
the viscous delirium you silence.

I've come
to look at your enigma.

I flee from everyone.

There'll be no good port
where you can moor the womb.

Acknowledgments

My gratitude to all those who helped *Unnameable* see through to its published form that you are now holding in your hands.

First and foremost, thank you, Anna Gual, for entrusting me with the translation of your work into English and our ensuing collaboration, and friendship.

I was thrilled to receive a National Endowment of the Arts Translation Fellowship for this work in 2022 and could thank Katy Day and her colleagues at the time endlessly for the vote of confidence, not to mention the financial breathing space the award afforded a debut poetry translator as myself.

A special shout out to the first US literary journal to take a chance on the work—poet-translator and editor Chloe Garcia Roberts, who, taking in my spiel at the 2022 AWP, agreed to review then publish a group of Anna Gual's poems and my English translations as part of the Omniglots Series at the *Harvard Review* (July 2022).

In December 2023, Contra Mundum Press' *Hyperion* magazine, under the stewardship of Rainer J. Hanshe, published, in their special edition on Catalan literature, not only some of my translations of Cebrià Montoliu's 1913 book on the life and work of Walt Whitman, but also a nine-poem portfolio of my translations of Anna's work. Thank you, Rainer, for this generous inclusion.

For the first Sant Jordi Festival USA, conceived and composed by Mary Ann Newman—under lockdown—as well as for versions 2023 and 2024, Anna and I contributed videos of our work. Thank you, Mary Ann, and all of the interns, for your indefatigable efforts stemming from and towards the discovery and appreciation of Catalan culture in the US and abroad.

A thank you to *Poetry*, for publishing in, and recording us for, the June 2023 issue, and for thus having Anna be the third Catalan poet and first female Catalan poet to be published in your pages.

A delightful thank you to Tess Barry and James Heaney of Carlow University, for inviting us that same June to present our work as part of the MFA residency program at Trinity College—on Bloomsday, and in the Samuel Beckett Room, no less!

Thank you, too, editors of the bilingual print magazine *Circumference* for publishing a trio of poems in your summer 2023 issue.

Appreciation to the team at the 2024 European Literary Festival, where Anna was a guest and where she presented five of her poems in Catalan and in my translations as part of the program.

Gratitude to the editors of *Four Way Review* who published our work in August 2024.

Thank you, Janani Ambikapathy, Editor of *Modern Poetry in Translation*, for accepting poems for *MPT*'s special issue on Catalan poetry, "Your Language Anticipating Mine," naming the issue after a line in one of Anna's poems, and for inviting me to participate in a podcast conversation with Ronald J. Puppo and Marilena Carr. Thank you, Ron, for letting me know *MPT* was planning this special issue.

This spring 2025, *Poetry International Online* published and recorded poems from Anna's oeuvre. A thank you to poet, translator, and editor Blas Falconer for this opportunity and to poet-translator and editorial intern Milagros Vilaplana for our fortuitous running into each other, figuratively and literally, and your appreciative ear, at the 2024 AWP.

Gratitude to Managing and Culture Editor Michelle Johnson and her enthusiasm for and acceptance of Anna's work for the September 2025 issue of *World Literature Today*.

Thank you poet-translator Allison deFreese and OSTI colleagues (Oregon Society of Translators and Interpreters) for having the perspicacity to jump on Zoom during the early days of the pandemic and for inviting me to share aloud, for the first time, my translations of Anna's poems.

Appreciation to poet-translator Kelsi Vanada and other ALTA contributors for giving Anna and I the Zoom opportunity to present together.

And for offering me concentrated time in community and in necessary solitude to advance this collection: residencies Cité internationale des arts (Paris); Faberllull (Olot); Millay Arts (NY); NES Artist Residency (Skagaströnd); Sundress Academy for the Arts (TN); and Write On, Door County (WI).

Una abraçada ben forta to the constellation of my Catalan and related colleagues and friends at the Universitat Autònoma de Barcelona, with deep appreciation to the director of my dissertation, and flowing knowledge fountain, Francesc Parcerisas; thank you, Toni R. Juncosa, poet-translator, for word insight and assurance; thank you to PEN Català, its community, past and present, and especially to Raffaella Salierno, a steadfast and joyful presence; to La Central, carrer d'Elisabets, where I first pulled down one of Anna's books from a poetry shelf, and was left floored, exhilarated, and determined; to l'Ateneu, its library and palm-forested café of calm and conversation; to The Institut Ramon Llull and its support; to Mireia Estrada, her understanding of a working, writing mother, and her welcoming residency JIWAR, and to Faberllull | Olot for their enthusiasm and faith. Thank you all for sharing of yourselves and Catalunya's cultural richness with me during these years.

Recognition and deep gratitude to Francesc Parcerisas and Jane Huffman for their time, close readings of the poems herein, and their respective impressions of what they discovered.

Thank you, family and friends, teachers all, for accompanying me, my work and my wonder.

Thank you, Reader, for your curiosity, and company.

Thank you to the following publications where some of these poems appeared, sometimes in varying forms:

Omniglots Series at the *Harvard Review*: Abundance, Descent, The Natural Occult, Estepa, Hypericum Balearicum.

Contra Mundum Press' *Hyperion*: Unnameable, Commotion, Millimeters, Chrome, Needing to Make a Hole, Inner Forest, Reader in the Grotto, Convalescence, Bread & Onion.

Poetry: Inner Journey.

Circumference: Chrome, Touch, Tactile.

Four Way Review: Profanity, The Evidence.

Modern Poetry in Translation: Re-re-re-besàvia / Great-great-great great grandmother, La petició / The petition (Note: Petition from *Les ocultacions*, its own collection apart from *Unnameable*).

MPT Podcast: https://modernpoetryintranslation.com/mpt-podcast-catalan-edition-ronald-puppo-speaks-to-kaiser-and-marialena-carr/

Poetry International Online: The Seed I, The Seed II, Clay (Note: All from *Les ocultacions*, its own collection apart from *Unnameable*).

Forthcoming in *World Literature Today*, September issue: Fail Better.

Contributors

Anna Gual is one of Catalonia's most vital poetic voices. Her quests, and the singular ways she embarks on and writes them, draw in poets, readers, and critics alike. She is the author of consistently prize-winning collections of poetry: *Implosions* (2008), *L'ésser solar* (2013), *Símbol 47* (2015), *Molsa* (2016), *El tubercle* (2016), *Altres semideus* (2019), *Ameba* (2020) and *Les ocultacions* (2022). Additionally, *Innombrable*, a selected works (2019) and, as editor, *Jo tinc mort petita* (2025). Poems have been translated into several languages and transposed into song. She regularly appears at European literary festivals and in 2021 was artist-in-residence at El Palau de la Música. Along with poet-translator and critic Jaume C. Pons Alorda, she created a reading series celebrating living Catalan poetry forerunners and peers. Collections have been translated into French, Italian, and Spanish. *Unnameable,* translated by AKaiser, is the first book of her work to appear in English. https://annagual.cat/

AKaiser holds a doctorate in Translation & Intercultural Studies, Universitat Autònoma de Barcelona, and is the Pushcart Prize-nominated author of *glint* (2020) and 2022 NEA Fellowship-awarded translator of Catalan, French, and Spanish. She holds a BA in Political Science from the University of Pennsylvania. Political and teaching work includes with UNESCO, UN-NYC, Spanish Mission to the UN, and in Europe and Latin America. Translations and translations-in-progress from Catalan include Anna Gual's recent book, *Les ocultacions*; Toni R. Juncosa's *El tel de l'elegia*, winner of the 2024 Francesc Garriga Poetry Prize; poems by Mireia Calafell and Miriam Cano; essays by Cebrià Montoliu, transatlantic urbanista, city-garden advocate, and the first Iberian translator of Emerson, Ruskin, and Whitman, about whom she is writing a biography; and writings by and on architect Antoni Gaudí. From Spanish, Mapuche composer and theorist, Anahí Mariluan, and Mexican poet Javier Acosta Escareño. https://akaiser.org